GET FIT FOR GROWTH

12 FUNDAMENTAL PRINCIPLES TO UNLEASH THE GROWTH POTENTIAL OF YOUR BUSINESS

Barbara Armstrong

Copyright © 2016 by St James Publishing. All rights reserved.

ISBN: 1534720464
ISBN 13: 9781534720466
Library of Congress Control Number: 2016910040
CreateSpace Independent Publishing Platform
North Charleston, South Carolina

Published by St James Publishing
152 City Road, London EC1V 2NX

No part of this publication may be reproduced, stored in a retrieval system, or transmitted in any form or by any means, electronic, mechanical, photocopying, recording, canning, or otherwise, without the prior written permission of the publisher.

Contents

Preface ································ vii

Acknowledgements ······················ ix

Introduction ··························· xi

Chapter 1　The Principle of Scalability: the journey from small to large ···················· 1

Chapter 2　The Principle of Change: there is no growth without change ················ 7

Chapter 3　The Principle of Leadership: The force behind business growth ················ 13

Chapter 4　The Principle of Clarity: overcome the identity crisis ························ 21

Chapter 5　The Principle of Uniqueness: stand out from the rest ························ 30

Chapter 6	The Principle of Focus: mapping the road to success · 39
Chapter 7	The Principle of Team: achieving more together· 45
Chapter 8	The Principle of Culture: Shaping attitudes, beliefs and behaviours· · · · · · · · · · · · · · · · · 52
Chapter 9	The Principle of Problem-Solving: moving forward unfettered · · · · · · · · · · · · · · · · · · · 57
Chapter 10	The Principle of Decision-Making: the power of choosing· 64
Chapter 11	The Principle of Innovation: driving business growth· 70
Chapter 12	The Principle of Risk Management: taking the leap · 77
	What Next? - Over to you · · · · · · · · · · · · · · 85
	About the Author · 87
	Notes· 89

Preface

You want to grow your business, but did you know that 94% of companies are unprepared, ill-equipped and unfit for growth?[1]

Despite the fact that small and medium-sized enterprises, regardless of their industry or geography, have growth ambitions, they are struggling to achieve their plans in the highly competitive, global, dynamic context in which they now operate. They are not fit or ready for growth and their efforts are not producing the results that they are seeking.

While small and medium-sized enterprises may have strategic growth plans, these plans are not being implemented due mainly to capability constraints within the company, lack of clarity and focus on growth priorities and indistinct competitive advantage.

To achieve their ambitions, small and medium-sized enterprises must first and foremost focus on developing the organisational capability and culture that will prepare them for growth.

In *Get Fit for Growth* I share with you 12 fundamental principles that, if applied, will help your business to unleash its growth potential and realise its growth aspirations.

Acknowledgements

Without the support, help and advice of my colleagues, family and friends this book would not have been possible. Thank you all very much. You will never know how much I appreciate your support.

Special thanks must go to Gregory Skeete who helped me to set and stick to an ambitious timetable for completing the book. He also took time out of his own busy schedule for growing his own business and authoring his third and fourth books to share our monthly 'accountability' calls.

Also to Dr Ichak Adizes and the Adizes Institute for the decades of knowledge and wisdom that has been imparted to me. Thanks also for permission to include the Corporate Lifecycles Diagram used in Chapter 1.

I also extend heartfelt thanks to my spiritual parents Apostle Lynroy C Scantlebury and Prophetess Heather E Scantlebury of World Harvest Ministries International for their prayers, encouragement and belief in me.

Most of all, my thanks go to my husband Henry Armstrong, my daughter Omara Harding and my business partner Catherine Johns whose quiet faith and confidence spurred me on.

INTRODUCTION

> *"There's no secret to success. It is the result of preparation, hard work and learning from failure"*
> — COLIN POWELL

This book has been more than a decade in the making. It is the result of working with and learning from the successes and failures of growth-focused business leaders and the experience of starting as well as growing my own business. I have come to realise that the reason so many growth plans do not materialise is because it takes more than a well-developed strategy and great ambition to successfully grow a business.

There is so much information available about productising, market research, market penetration strategies, alternative selling channels, opportunity analysis, segmentation strategy, acquisition strategies… it can make your head spin. However, very few sources, if any, tell you that these strategies only work when you have made sure that you have a strong foundation to build on the fundamental elements that must be in place before you embark on your growth journey.

Please don't get me wrong. There are some brilliant strategies that you should definitely embrace and you absolutely have to address the issues listed above. However, experience has taught me that if the ground isn't properly prepared, the seed won't grow!

Get Fit for Growth is all about preparing the ground.

By addressing some, if not all, of the 12 principles in this book, you will exponentially increase your chances of successfully growing your business. You will be better placed, better informed and better equipped to select and implement the right strategies for growth.

Preparing your business to move to the next phase of growth is about recognising that "what got you here won't get you there"[2]. It requires a 'next level' mind-set, a change of leadership approach and a change of operations to get you to where you want to be.

I have learnt that there are some fundamental principles that must also be in place to guarantee success and my aim is to help you identify the areas that you must tackle if you are serious about business growth.

Why I wrote this book

I am committed to helping busy, overstretched leaders to develop their skills, solve problems and build successful, profitable businesses – that is why I have written this book.

If you're not growing, you are dying.

I learnt this from Dr. Ichak Adizes PhD[3] whose business principles and methodologies have been successfully applied in thousands of companies all over the world for more than 40 years.

I am yet to meet a business leader who does not want their business to grow in some way – quality, turnover, efficiency, effectiveness or geographical area of operation – but, of course, it is not always easy in the current climate.

I know from experience of starting and growing my own businesses that it is a tough old world and when resources are limited or stretched, it is important to know where to invest and to get it right - preferably the first time.

Before you read on, let me be clear. I believe that business is not only about increasing your turnover and profitability. It is also about progressing and improving all the time in order to remain relevant and to successfully compete in a changing global marketplace.

Money and profits will come when you focus on the principles that make your business fit for growth.

Why it is so hard to grow a business?
Clearly, business leaders know about growth strategies (at least most of them that I have met) and lots of them have impressive plans. Yet quite often, these plans materialise only partially or not at all.

I have found after over a decade of working with more than 200 businesses that quite often it is not about the quality of the growth plans; it is the foundations that they are building on that impact the ability to grow. We all know that if we want a building to last, to withstand the storms, then it must be built upon strong, firm foundations. The same principles apply to business growth.

What is this book about?
This book is about helping you to understand what you need to have in place before you can successfully embark on your business growth journey.

Think about it as if it were a car. While the vehicle is designed to get you to where you want to be, it's not going to succeed if there is no petrol, the tyres are flat, the starter motor isn't firing or there's no oil to lubricate the engine.

Basically, if the foundations for growing your business are weak, then no matter how great your strategies are and how hard you work, the chances of success in both the short and long term are severely limited. (That's a polite way of saying – it won't work!)

How can this book help you?
I have sought in this book to identify and share with you what, in my experience, are some of the foundational principles that must be in place to make sure your business is fit for growth. I cannot claim that I have identified every single principle, but these 12 principles have consistently proved to be essential over the years. Applying these principles will definitely reap rewards and increase the potential for success in realising your business goals.

Who is this book for?
If you are an entrepreneur, an intrapreneur, the founder, owner or leader of a small or medium-sized private company or social enterprise then you will find something in this book for you.

How to Use this Book
The book is designed so that you can dip into the different principles that will be of most value to you. Nevertheless, I would urge you to read the first two principles because they are the foundation for the rest of the book.

Also, where you are in the Corporate Lifecycle (See Chapter 1) will determine which of these principles you need to place most emphasis on or put most energy into.

Each chapter of the book explores a separate business growth principle beginning with a brief context for the principle and ending with concluding thoughts and actions that you can take to address each of the principles in this book.

CHAPTER 1

THE PRINCIPLE OF SCALABILITY: THE JOURNEY FROM SMALL TO LARGE

> *"A web browser for parrots isn't meant to serve a scalable business market"*
>
> NEIL GERSHENFELD

"If we build it, they will come" is what one business owner said to me when I asked him about how he planned to realise his goal of taking the business from £2 to £5 million ($2.9 to $7.3) turnover.

As you can imagine, I was a little dismayed, to say the least.

The quote he used is derived from a movie called Field of Dreams[1] starring Kevin Costner.

In the movie a baseball-playing ghost (Ray Liotta) appears in Costner's cornfield and encourages him to plough it up in order to build a baseball field so that his childhood hero would appear.

After this encounter, Costner decides to follow the advice of the ghost, destroying the field, risking bankruptcy, loss of his livelihood and eviction from his farm.

It was a great film and, like most movies, there was a happy ending. However, this is not an approach that I would recommend. Pursuing an idea without, at minimum, testing that there is sustainable market for it, is not a business strategy. In the real world of business, knowing that you have a product or service that customers will buy is the first principle of growth.

Across the world, businesses are focused on growth, but growing a business is a challenge in this new dynamic, fast-paced, global environment, especially for small and medium-sized enterprises. However, growth is achievable if the organisation is properly prepared, fit and ready to meet the challenges.

The first step on the journey from small to large is to ensure that the business model is scalable.

What is scalability?

A business can be described as scalable if there is repeatable, predictable, sustainable demand for its products and services and if the business has the internal capacity to adjust to meet that demand profitably.

In addition to focusing on market demand and the capacity to meet it, the business needs to continue to profit in its current markets. This means that there should not be any decline in turnover or the ability of the business to sustain a high level of customer satisfaction and product quality at current or improved levels whilst the organisation is also pursuing a growth strategy.

Is your business scalable?
The first thing to determine before embarking on the journey towards growth is whether or not your business and business model are scalable.

It may seem obvious, but some business leaders are so committed to and excited about the prospect of growth, it is inconceivable to them that there may not be a large enough market for their product or service.

The quote for this chapter is a wonderful articulation of what it means to make sure that there is a market for your product or service. After all, I cannot imagine that there would be even one parrot in the world capable of browsing the Internet in order to make that business viable.

On the other hand, an example of a company that understood scalability is HP. When they found that the market for their printers was shrinking, they realised that they could make money selling printer cartridges instead.

If you are seeking business growth, you need to do your homework by making sure that there is a real and large enough market for your products and services. If you are depending on finding one parrot to browse your website, you could be disappointed.

This does not mean that growth is only achievable in a mass market with a high volume of sales. A scalable business model can also be a low-quantity exclusive market. Just as in a mass market, there is extensive scope for scale within an exclusive, luxury market. For example, Rolls Royce needs to sell one Phantom Coupe retailing at £492,000 ($696,660) and Mercedes-Benz has to sell 17 of its A Class model, retailing at £ 40,695 ($57,624) to generate the same income. Both are in the luxury market but differ in the number of sales required to sustain market share.

It is also about truly understanding your core competence and being able to parlay that into an array of different products, services and markets.

What is important is that there is a substantial enough market to make your business viable and you must have detailed knowledge and understanding of your specific market to determine whether or not your business is scalable.

Developing a scalable business model

The secret to success lies in the ability to develop a business model that is highly scalable and able to maintain accelerated growth. As illustrated in the diagram below, the four imperatives for developing your scalable business model are:

1. Offers a product or service that is related to the mission of the business
2. Delivers high value to the target customer (for example, ease of use or effectiveness)

3. Has the potential for secure repeat income from the target market
4. Operates in a sizeable market

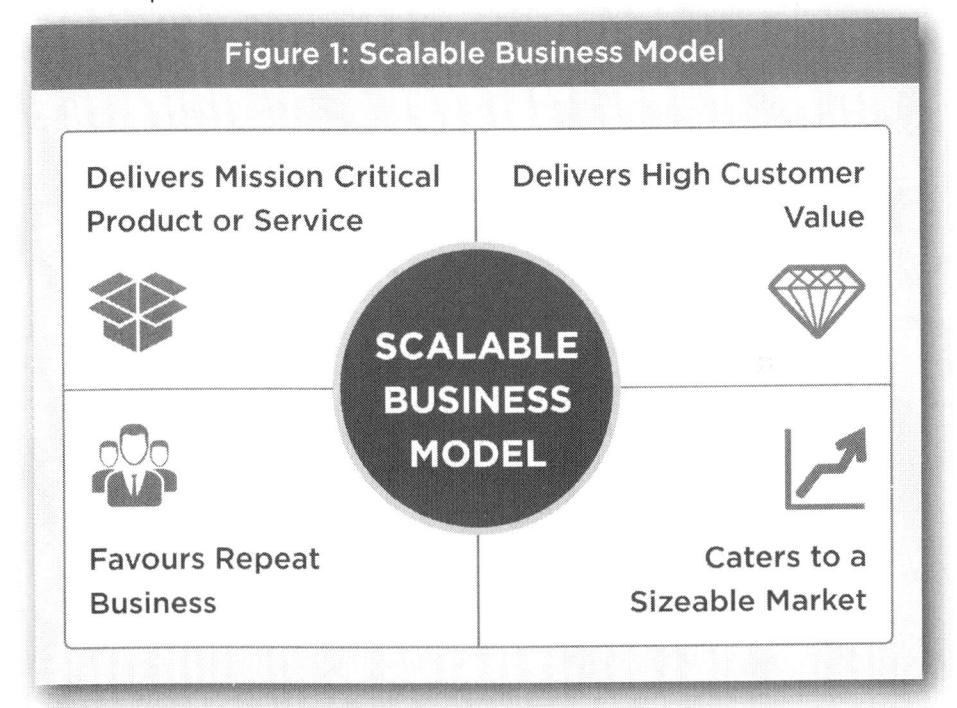

Figure 1: Scalable Business Model

Delivers Mission Critical Product or Service	Delivers High Customer Value
Favours Repeat Business	Caters to a Sizeable Market

SCALABLE BUSINESS MODEL

Concluding Thoughts

Before embarking on your growth journey, consider the 10 questions below to assist you in determining whether or not your business model is scalable:

1) What makes your product/service different from other providers in your market?
2) Are you delivering mission-critical products/services to your target market?

3) Do you deliver high value (versus price) to your target market?
4) Is the market large enough to withstand contraction?
5) Can your business generate repeat revenue from existing and potential customers?
6) Does the model generate positive cash flow?
7) Can the business grow organically from its own profits?
8) Is it feasible to grow the business with moderate investment in people and processes?
9) Do you market product or service offerings with a primary focus on outcomes for your customers?
10) Is your sales and marketing process agile and dynamic to reflect changing market conditions?

Although these questions on their own cannot provide a definitive answer to the question of whether or not you have a scalable business, they do go a long way towards raising awareness of what is required so that you can make an informed decision about your business model and potential for growth.

If, after addressing these questions, you believe that your business model and market are scalable, you are in a good position to begin preparation for the business to grow and for applying the **Get Fit for Growth** principles set out in subsequent chapters of this book.

CHAPTER 2

The Principle of Change: There is no Growth Without Change

> *"Life is a progress, not a station"*
> Ralph Waldo Emerson

Can you think of a single example of growth in any sphere of life where change is not the prerequisite?

- To grow from a child to an adult is about change
- For a caterpillar to transform into a butterfly it must change
- A seed rooted in the ground changes into a plant
- Learning something new develops and transforms our thinking and behaviours

Whether in business or in our personal lives, everything is subject to change and change is necessary if growth is desired. Of the 12 principles in this book, understanding the correlation between growth and change is conceivably the most significant.

Achieving growth in any business, large or small, requires change in thinking, change in being and change in doing. This means that for your business to successfully grow everyone from top to bottom must understand, be equipped for and contribute to the process of change.

Change Management Methodology

Much of my approach to change management when working with my clients is based on the work of Dr Ichak Adizes PhD and I am a Certified Change Leader, trained by the Adizes Institute.

I truly believe that these tried, tested and proven change methodologies are the best I have come across and I am continually looking for new and better ways to do things.

In this chapter, I will share some of the most insightful and essential Adizes philosophies that underpin effective business growth.

Understanding the nature of change

Over the past five to ten years the world of business has changed dramatically.

Companies of all shapes, sizes and in any sector – public, private or not-for-profit - are able to operate on an international basis because of technological advances. Entrepreneurs are emerging from every corner of the globe. Millennials are more motivated by contribution than they are by financial reward. Customers have far more choice than ever before and expect the highest standards and quality of service.

In this rapid, connected, global context, only businesses that are nimble, adaptable, imaginative and brutally self-aware can successfully compete, grow and thrive.

This is the backdrop against which businesses are now operating. Hence the need to understand that change is not only a constant, but also its swiftness has increased and its impact is global.

Adizes also expounds the concept of change as a cycle – a continuous loop. In other words, change breeds change. Therefore, whether change is instigated internally or imposed from the outside, the implication is that one change leads to more change and this is continuous, never-ending, unremitting.

I always tell the leaders that I work with that this is their reality. That there are no strategies, no matter how well resourced, that they could put in place to eradicate change. It is a fact of life and a fact of business that must be embraced. To do anything but embrace it is to open the door to stagnation and decline from which it is not easy to recover.

Everything has a Lifecycle

More than 40 years of research, knowledge and experience has proved that businesses have a lifecycle, just like any living organism.

Organisations therefore follow predictable patterns of birth, growth, aging and death. However, there is one emphatic difference. Organisations do not **have to** age and die. It is possible for them to remain perpetually young and vital.

This peak state, referred to as "Prime", is where organisations find a balance between being efficient and effective in the short and long term. It is this balance that results in organisational vitality.

Progressing from one stage of the Adizes Corporate Lifecycle (illustrated in figure 2) to the next demands change; change in approach, change in focus, change in leadership style, change in decisions and actions.

To reach and sustain the position of Prime on the Adizes Corporate Lifecycle: Managing Corporate Lifecycles[2] requires focus, commitment and work. It cannot be achieved or prolonged without deliberate decisions and actions. Neither can it be prolonged by believing that the actions the organisation took in the past will ensure success in the future. It is a dynamic state.

Figure 2: The Adizes Corporate Lifecycle

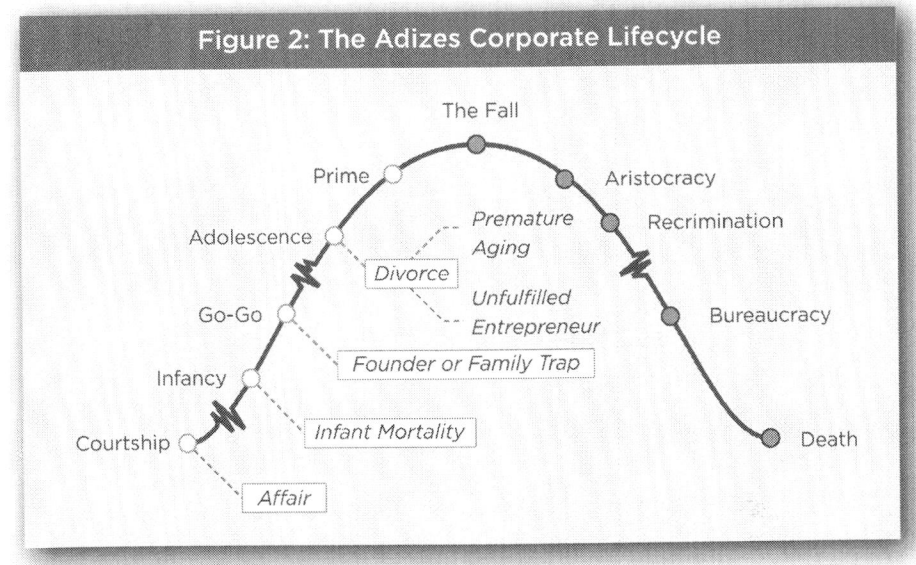

- Courtship
- Infancy
- Go-Go
- Adolescence
- Prime
- The Fall
- Aristocracy
- Recrimination
- Bureaucracy
- Death

Failure modes: Affair, Infant Mortality, Founder or Family Trap, Unfulfilled Entrepreneur, Divorce, Premature Aging

© Ichak Adizes 1979: Managing Corporate Lifecycles

To be a Prime business it is necessary to continuously focus on:

- Producing results for your customers
- Administering your human and financial resources wisely
- Evaluating and assessing the changing environment that you operate in
- Innovating to grow
- Having the right people, with the right skills, in the right place, doing the right things
- Being open to inspiration, but having the rigour to assess viability of that inspiration

Concluding Thoughts

At each stage of growth and development the amount of energy you put into producing results, administering resources, innovating and people development will vary, but the one thing that you cannot avoid – if you are to grow your business – is the need to change!

In this context, the Henry Ford quote, "If you always do what you've always done, you'll always get what you've always got"[2] is not true, certainly not in terms of business growth. If you do what you always did you will quickly start to lose competitive advantage, market share will erode and the business will not be viable.

What do you think happened to the businesses on the right-hand side of the Lifecycle diagram? I imagine that they continued to do what they always did and thought that their history, reputation and past success would keep them at their peak. Clearly this wasn't the case.

CHAPTER 3

THE PRINCIPLE OF LEADERSHIP: THE FORCE BEHIND BUSINESS GROWTH

> *"It's hard to lead a cavalry charge if you think you look funny on a horse"*
> ADLAI E STEVENSON II

If change is the car that will take your business on the journey towards growth, then leadership is the engine that powers it. Business growth demands leadership excellence that inspires and encourages others to believe that success is possible.

For over a decade I have worked with business leaders – some good, some not so good and some truly outstanding. Those that are outstanding are also successful in developing and growing their businesses. They succeed because they inspire creativity, align relationships, create a positive organisational culture and invest resources in the development of human, operational, financial and managerial capability.

They display entrepreneurial leadership characteristics that I will share with you in this chapter and most of which can be developed and honed over time.

One of the leaders that I have worked with for almost 8 years exemplifies the leadership excellence explored in this chapter. Year on year she invests in the development of her staff, allocates time and money for them to review operational effectiveness and encourages them to forward ideas for improving services or creating products.

Entrepreneurial Leadership

In this increasingly dynamic, turbulent and globally competitive environment, business growth requires a new type of entrepreneurial leader that is distinct from the managerial leader.

Not only do entrepreneurial leaders create a compelling vision, they instil in their employees and colleagues the confidence to think and behave entrepreneurially. Figure 3 summarises some of the main qualities of the entrepreneurial leader:

Figure 3: The Entrepreneurial Leader

- Visionary
- Change Leader
- People Leader
- Innovator
- Systemic Thinker
- Entrepreneurial Leader (center)

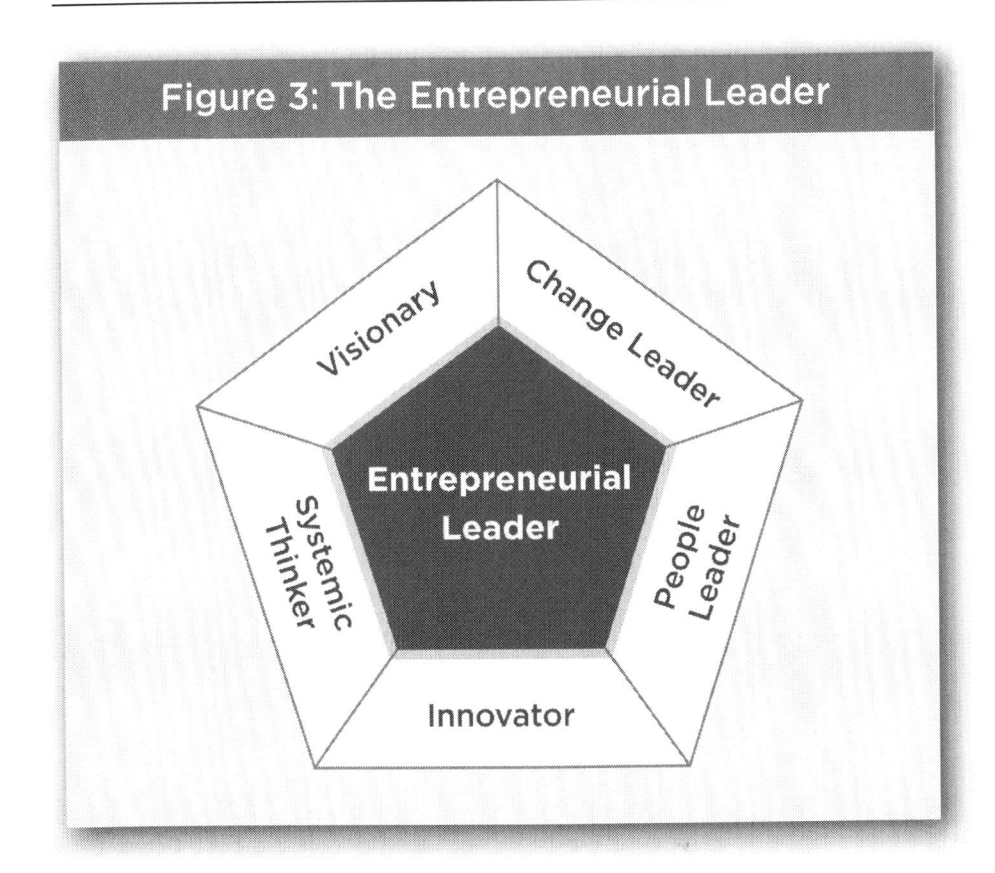

An Entrepreneurial Mind-set

It is surprising how many leaders approach growth as a purely strategic exercise without addressing the essential paradigm shift in thinking required to successfully lead growth. An entrepreneurial mind-set is about setting the strategic vision and direction, encouraging creativity and innovation, searching continually for opportunities, venturing into new areas and creating value.

Listed below are twelve important examples of an entrepreneurial mind-set that you can assess yourself against to determine your areas of strength and those that you may wish to develop:

1. Belief in your own ability and the ability of the organisation to succeed
2. An obsessive focus on the customer
3. Passion and excitement for seeking out new opportunities
4. Tolerance of ambiguity
5. Courage to try new things and take risks
6. Perseverance and a dogged determination to succeed
7. Decisiveness – making speedy and effective decisions
8. Self-discipline, clarity and focus on the goal
9. Resilience and bounce-back-ability
10. Adapting readily to and embracing change
11. Inspiring others to greatness
12. Boundless optimism

Keep a positive attitude

Often, statements that we make or that are made by the people around us can easily stir up negative feelings and thoughts, and impact on our minds. Often, it is far easier to accept a negative thought than it is to accept a positive one.

Having a positive attitude is not about pie-in-the-sky thinking. It is about seeing things in perspective and framing them in a positive light. The right attitude embraces challenges and always looks for the lesson buried in the difficulties.

Learn from failure

Failure and disappointment can be difficult, but they are also great learning opportunities. Instead of being ashamed of the mistakes you have made, seek the lessons you can learn from these mistakes. By learning from mistakes you grow stronger. Each one of those experiences helps shape you as an individual and create a mind-set that is open to change.

Entrepreneurship coach Ajaero Tony Martins puts it like this: "Underneath every mistake in business is a valuable lesson. Unfortunately, many entrepreneurs miss these lessons because they lament and blame others over the mistakes."[1]

Stand out from the crowd

Entrepreneurs embrace their distinctiveness. Sometimes we may want to blend in rather than be obviously different. However, as an entrepreneurial leader you need to embrace what distinguishes you from others. When you celebrate what makes you and your company different, you stand out from the crowd and from your competitors.

It is also worth noting that although there is a school of thought that introverts cannot be entrepreneurs, it is not a view that I subscribe to. I have worked with entrepreneurial leaders who have a variety of styles and many introverts who are as successful as extroverts, if not more successful.

Embrace continuous learning

The quickest way to stagnation is to reject new modes of thinking. Entrepreneurial leaders are defined by their ability to expand their thinking and embrace new technology, theories and practices.

An unending appetite for new learning feeds the entrepreneurial mind-set and enhances the skills that will ultimately help you to grow your business.

Pace yourself

As an entrepreneurial leader, you have a lot you need to accomplish to achieve your business dreams. Although perseverance is an entrepreneurial trait, you need to pace yourself as you pursue success. Pushing yourself and putting in the hours may be admirable qualities, but ultimately it is unsustainable and unhealthy in the long term for you, your family and the business.

Rather than the focus on work-life balance that has been promulgated for many years, I believe entrepreneur and hedge fund manager, James Altucher, provides excellent advice in his book, *The Choose Yourself Guide to Wealth*: "...everything in your life is connected including the physical, emotional, mental and spiritual...take care of these four areas of your life every single day without fail."[2]

Yeah! I reject the work-life balance dichotomy – it's all life and I choose to do what I enjoy and what fulfils me as a person.

Follow through
If you've ever attended a networking event and met people who promise to call you but never do, you see the lost opportunity of not following through. Think of following through as grabbing an opportunity. You never know which one of your efforts will succeed and following through is just another way of being proactive — call people back, reach out to colleagues, respond to emails and messages as soon as possible.

Be goal driven
Entrepreneurial leaders understand what their priorities are and work towards their goals consistently. If the objective is business growth, the quality of the goals you set must be high. You must think at a higher level and be more ambitious than you have been before.

Steward Leadership
Great leadership is also about long-term stewardship. Not only must leaders seek to protect shareholder interests, they must also be custodians of the organisational culture, of the human and financial resources and of the company's impact on the environment. Ultimately, a growth-focused leader combines corporate and social responsibility with effectiveness in the management of resources.

Concluding Thoughts
A global study by Egon Zehnder International and McKinsey & Co[3] identified a direct correlation between leadership talent

and business growth, citing these 5 competencies as most important for growth:

- Developing organisational capability – a systematic focus on developing critical skills throughout the organisation
- Team leadership – the ability to focus, align and build high-performing teams
- Change leadership – the ability to drive large-scale, coordinated change across the entire organisation
- Market insight – the ability to look beyond the company's current context to discern future growth opportunities
- Results orientation – the ability to lead and transform a business for high performance

There is no end of opportunity to develop the leadership skills that will enable you to take the business to the next level, including:

- Executive coaching
- Leadership programmes
- Peer group membership
- Reading leadership books
- Finding a mentor
- Membership of an external board

You should be as fully committed to your development as you are to the development of others in the business.

CHAPTER 4

THE PRINCIPLE OF CLARITY: OVERCOME THE IDENTITY CRISIS

> "**Mystification is simple; clarity is the hardest thing of all**"
>
> JULIAN BARNES

In *Alice in Wonderland*[4], Alice daydreams during her history lesson. She reflects on the kind of world she would create and contemplates "…everything would be nonsense. Nothing would be what is because everything would be what it isn't."

Sometimes I see similar thought processes in the leaders that I work with. They know in their own minds how they want the world to be, what they want to achieve and even how they want to do it. The problem is that it is only clear to them and not to everyone else – especially the people that they need to help them create the world that they envisage.

More often I meet leaders who are not sure what the vision is for growth. They simply know that "we need to grow" and wonder why nothing is happening. They struggle to articulate the why, what, who and how of the business. They have an identity crisis.

The world that Alice dreamt of can be understood, but it would be easier and quicker to grasp if she said: "I imagine a world full of wonder, surprise and adventure, where nothing is as you would expect it to be".

The principle of clarity focuses on defining what your business is about, its purpose and what problems it is solving in the world. When you are clear about why the business exists, where you want to be and what you want to achieve, the chances of success are increased exponentially.

During this chapter, we will focus on clearly defining your business' **purpose**, **mission** and **vision**. These three key elements are essential to know where your business is now and where it is intending to head so that your growth activities are aligned and everyone in the business understands their contribution to reaching your destination.

Purpose – 'Start with the Why'

Many business owners and leaders believe that their business' purpose is to maximise profits and improve cash flow, and to provide a return on the shareholders' investment (or a surplus for reinvestment in the case of not-for-profit organisations). But profits are an outcome, a result, a reflection or achievement, not the purpose for which the organisation exists.

Why does your business exist?
As a result of research into the success of the world's most influential brands, Simon Sinek, author, speaker and consultant who writes on leadership and management, demonstrates the importance of 'why' in developing and growing a business.

Sinek asked companies why their customers choose them and the majority determined that it was their fantastic, keenly priced and great quality products or services. In other words, **what** they do and **how** they do it.

In his book Start with the Why[5], Sinek explains that the customer is actually driven much more by the "why" than the "what" and "how" of the company.

He discovered that successful, growing companies begin with why, and then focus on how before determining what. He describes this as The Golden Circle, as illustrated in the diagram below:

Figure 4: Simon Sinek's Golden Circle

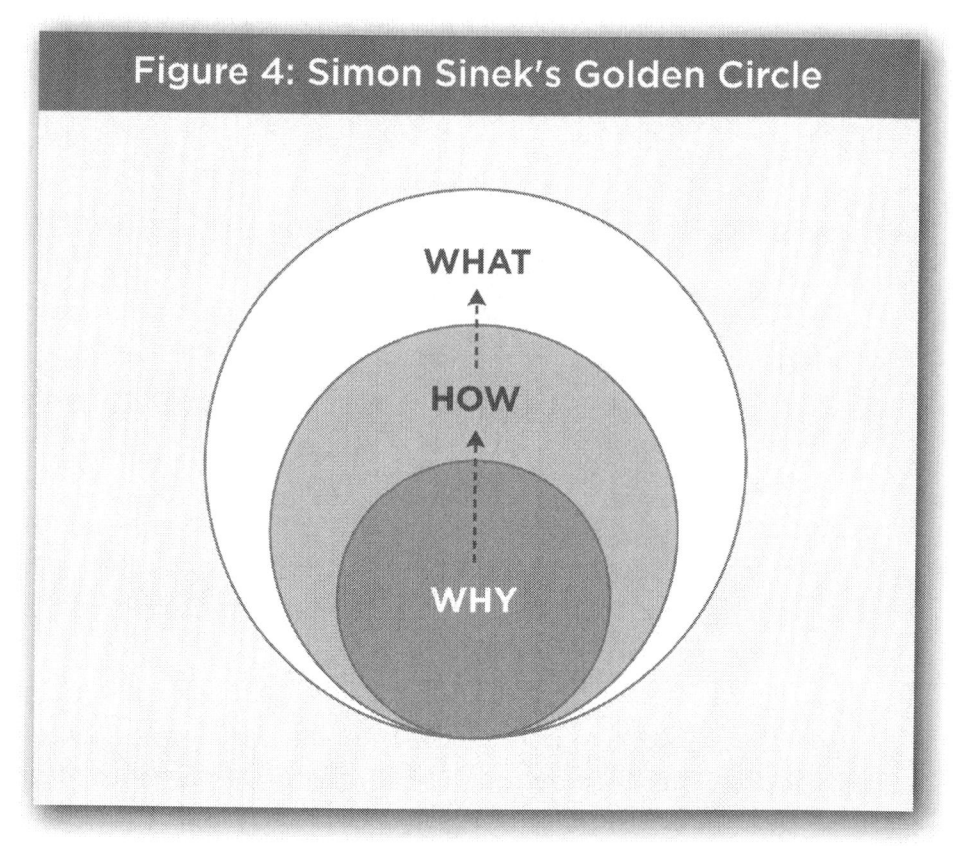

The Golden Circle can be compared to the human brain:

- The **What** is likened to the neocortex, relating to the rational, analytical and language part of the brain
- The **How** and the **Why** are likened to the limbic system. This is a part of the brain that responds to emotions such as trust and loyalty and is responsible for all human behaviour and decision-making

When businesses start by communicating **what** they do, they are appealing to the customer's neocortex, the rational. However, this does not drive their behaviour and decision-making – the limbic system does. Sinek therefore urges us to make this our starting point, the core of our approach.

The result of applying this approach to defining the business purpose is to create a single, clear, consistent message that inspires, motivates and engenders loyalty and effective decision-making in customers and employees alike.

Sinek uses the example of Apple to effectively convey this model:

- **Why** – to challenge the status quo by thinking differently
- **How** and **What** – they challenge the status quo by making products with an eye-catching design that are easy to use

Henry Ford was an excellent example of someone who focused on the 'why' with his now famous apocryphal, "If I'd listened to customers, I would have built a faster horse."

What is the *Why* of your business?
When you are clear about the **Why** of your business, it becomes much easier to communicate this in your Mission and Vision statements.

Your Mission and Vision Statements
Over the years I have often been asked what the difference is between mission and vision statements, how they should be written and why it is important to have them at all.

My response is that they are valuable because well-defined mission and vision statements form the backbone of your strategic plan and provide a roadmap to success.

A Management Tools Insight by Bain and Company[6] indicates that organisations that have clearly defined mission and vision statements that are aligned with a strategic plan outperform those that do not.

What is the difference between a mission and vision statement?

The **Vision Statement** is about the future of your business.

The **Mission Statement** tells you what you are doing today that will take you where you want to go in the future. See Figure 5 below:

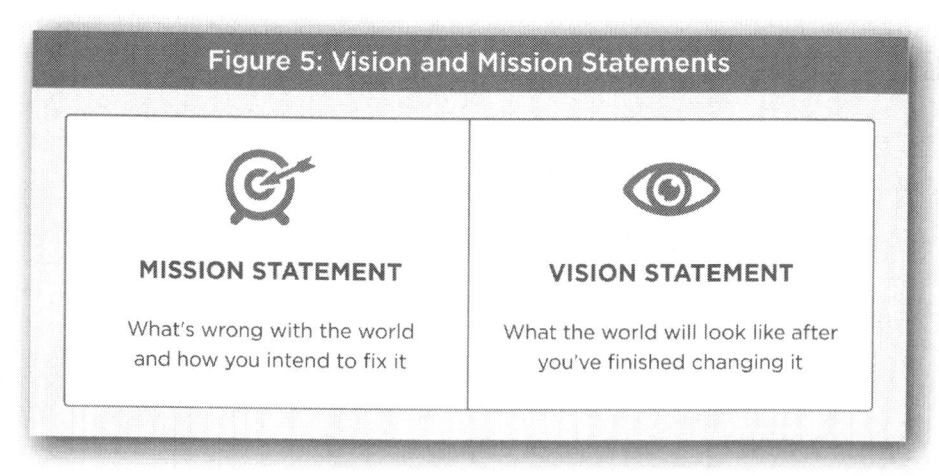

Figure 5: Vision and Mission Statements

MISSION STATEMENT	VISION STATEMENT
What's wrong with the world and how you intend to fix it	What the world will look like after you've finished changing it

Mission Statement

Your company's Mission Statement is your opportunity to define the strategic goals, business improvement, ethics and culture. It is also a template for decision-making.

The mission statement keeps everyone clear on the direction of the business and helps people who may be uncomfortable or resistant to more readily understand and embrace change.

Even if you do not have a team of employees, a mission statement is invaluable.

The best mission statements define a company's goals in the following dimensions:

1. What the company does for its customers;
2. What it does for its employees;
3. What it does for its owners;
4. What it does for its community and
5. What it does for the world

Mission is to the company what a map is to a traveller, a rudder to a ship, a blueprint to an architect. It provides a framework for thinking throughout the business.

What does your Mission Statement say about your business?

Vision Statement

John Kotter's article in Forbes, "When CEOs Talk Strategy, 70% Of the Company Doesn't Get It"[7], contends that few employees understand the company's strategy. This results in poor decision-making at all levels of an organisation. For that reason, the first step towards crafting a vision statement is to take a careful look at where you are as a company, your place in the industry, the opportunities for growth in the market for the intermediate and long term, and the capability of the business to pursue opportunities.

A carefully crafted vision statement can help to communicate your company's goals to employees and customers in a single sentence or a few concise paragraphs. Vision statements should be aspirational, stating the most important primary goals for your company.

Outlining the key objectives for the business enables employees to feel confident in putting forward ideas, taking independent action and developing strategies to achieve the stated goals. With a single vision statement, employees are all on the same page and will be more productive.

Concluding Thoughts

If you are trying to expand your business you can ask yourself the following questions:

- Am I clearly communicating the company's vision and mission?
- Are our incentives aligned with business goals?
- Do the vision and mission statements show clients and prospective clients how we differ from our competitors?
- Are we thinking big enough?

- Do the vision and mission statements help us to attract the right staff?
- How do the vision and mission statements contribute to creating a positive organisational culture?

It is helpful to explore these questions with members of your management team and staff teams to reinforce a culture of engagement, participation and consultation.

CHAPTER 5

THE PRINCIPLE OF UNIQUENESS: STAND OUT FROM THE REST

> "**Your uniqueness is your ultimate strength**"
> DEBASISH MRIDHA, MD

When I started my business almost twelve years ago, I had great support and guidance from a variety of experienced, successful entrepreneurs. One consistent piece of advice was to make sure that I gave customers a reason to buy from me instead of someone else.

This was great advice, because a business needs to define its uniqueness to differentiate it from its competitors. Based on this experience, I always ask this question of the leaders that I work with when I am helping them to develop their business strategies: "What is unique about your business that would make a customer buy from you instead of someone else?"

Often, I find that they struggle to answer this question. However, it is imperative because it is an essential part of your strategy and your ability to create the context for business growth.

Every business needs a unique statement that informs customers who you are, what you do and defines how you differ from your competitors. Some companies also use the statement slogan.

Identifying your uniqueness also aligns with your Vision, Mission and Purpose.

You will discover that taking the time to define your uniqueness can also help you to uncover some new products or services that you can bring to the market to grow your business.

In this chapter we explore approaches to developing your uniqueness.

What is a Unique Selling Point?

A unique selling point (USP) is the way you define your company's unique position in the marketplace. This is often overlooked when growing a business, but creating a business that customers love is a guaranteed formula for success.

If prospective customers are finding it difficult to decide between your product or service and your competitor's, a strong USP will distinguish your business and actively focus your energy on creating products that cater to your target market.

A strong USP makes you stand out from your competitors and helps you to focus your energy and efforts on creating and delivering products and services that cater to your target market.

Over the years I have realised that while a superior product and outstanding service are the foundation for growing a company, there is an opportunity to use differentiation as a competitive advantage. In essence, it is about defining what your business has to offer that your competitors do not.

According to Coaching by Subject Experts (CBSE) website[1], "there is nothing more mission-critical than your USP 'Unique Selling Proposition' for your business" and the importance of this is illustrated in the diagram below:

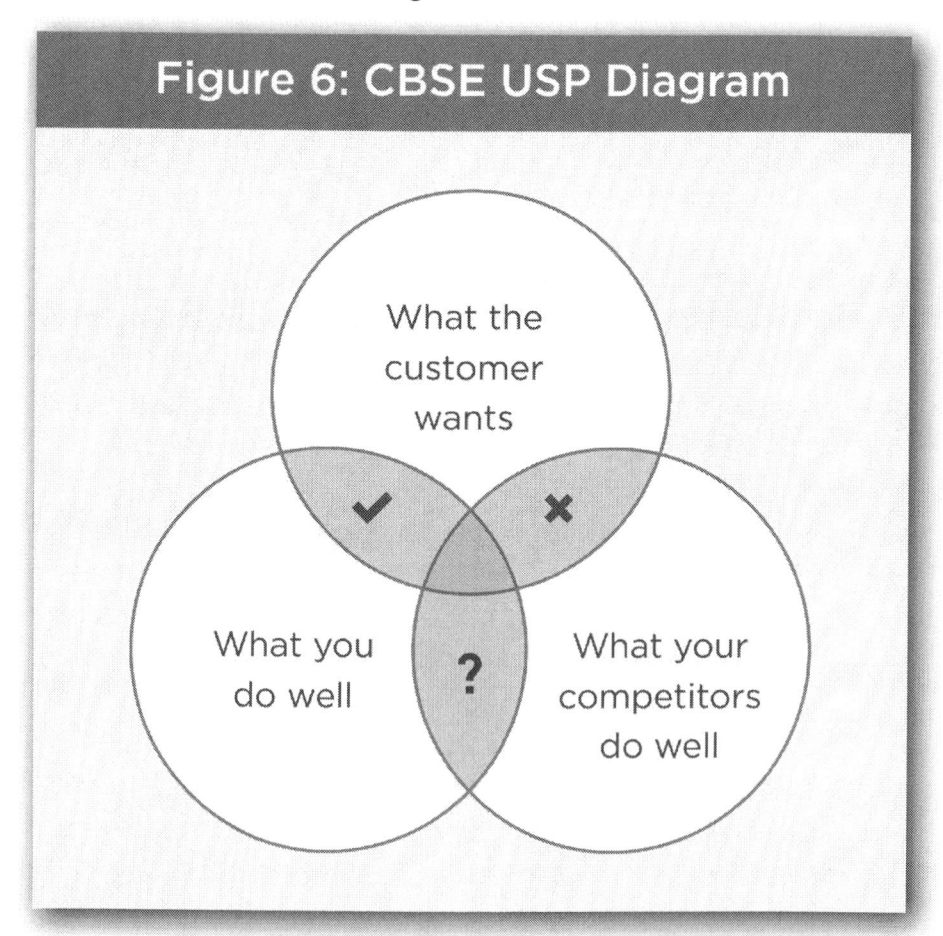

Figure 6: CBSE USP Diagram

- What the customer wants
- What you do well
- What your competitors do well

As you can see from the graphic, there is a "Winning Zone", symbolised by (✓), where your USP comes into play. This is the intersection between the capabilities of the business and the opportunity to meet the needs of your customers in your market. In this zone there is a clear point of differentiation where you are uniquely placed to meet the needs of the customer.

The "Losing Zone" symbolised by (✗), is the intersection between what the customer wants and what your competitors do well. In this zone your competitors can meet the needs of your customer better than you do.

The third area is the "Risk Zone", symbolised by (?). It is known as the competitive battleground. This is the zone where the business must both innovate and execute at a superior level to successfully grow.

Your USP Attributes

It is imperative to build a business on your unique attributes.

In some instances it is a combination of attributes that makes your business different and there are numerous attributes that can define your USP, as you will see from the examples below:

1. **Product** - you can provide a unique product or expand an existing product to make it more useful to the customer;
2. **Service** – the same applies for a service offering. You can offer a unique service or expand a service;

3. **Market Niche** – you can carve out a unique niche in your industry and become the most dominant player in that industry;
4. **Offer** - you can become known for a unique offer that only you are making in your market;
5. **Solve a Problem** – identify a specific problem that prospects in your market are experiencing and offer a solution;
6. **Added Value**- you could give your customers extras that our competitors do not provide. It is important to demonstrate the added value to the customer;
7. **Guarantee** – you could offer a warranty or guarantee so strong that it sets your business apart from all the rest;
8. **Customer Service** – give your customer more than they expect or that you have promised. The old adage of "under promise and over deliver" is as true today as it always was;
9. **Intellectual Property** – your company may boast a unique product or service, combination with experience, expertise that differentiates you in the marketplace.

This is not an exhaustive list, but provides a sound basis to begin developing your USP. What other unique attributes do you have or could you develop to differentiate your business in your marketplace?

Creating Your USP

Once you have identified the attributes that distinguish your business, it is time to create your USP. For clients who continue to struggle with the concept of identifying their USP, I advise a number of strategies, including:

1. **Ask your customers** - they can tell you why they chose you, why they stay and why they refer;
2. **Involve your staff** – use an experienced facilitator for a fun, creative thinking session to identify your USP attributes;
3. **Know your target market** – create an avatar of your ideal customer. Be specific about who they are and what problem you are solving for them and create your USP based on them;
4. **Study your competitors** – take a close look at the closest competitors in your market. What do they offer? How do they position themselves?
5. **Study the USP of others** – find, study and model the best USPs in the market to help you construct your own;
6. **Think of a promise** - when you think of your USP as your promise to your clients it becomes easier to identify your differentiators.

Once you find your unique attribute or combination of attributes to differentiate your business, come up with a strong statement and image that convey your USP. All of your advertising and promotion should be centred on communicating your USP.

Value Proposition

Value Proposition and Unique Selling Point are often confused and some question whether both are needed.

According to a definition by Jill Konarth[2], your Value Proposition is "a clear statement of the tangible results a customer gets from your products or services".

On the other hand, your Unique Selling Point, as explained earlier, is what differentiates a product or service from other similar products or services.

A Value Proposition should make your prospective customer pay attention to your product or service.

Jill Konarth, who has written some excellent blogs and articles about sales strategies and techniques, identifies 3 primary components for developing value propositions that customers can relate to:

1. Testimonials – a testimonial from a satisfied customer can really capture attention. Happy customers are usually eager to provide testimonials, but rarely do so of their volition. Ensure that you ask for their feedback.
2. Statistics – use both client and industry statistics. If you can collate statistics to demonstrate the positive outcomes for your customers, you are able to quantify the value of your product or service. If you are using industry statistics, make sure that they are from credible sources and are not over-used or clichéd in your industry. Take time to do your research and use statistics that your competitors are not using.
3. Language – use language that your customer relates to. Avoid using sales, marketing or product knowledge words. Your product or service features and benefits

are unlikely to be the language that your prospective customers use.

Concluding Thoughts

I recently heard the leader of a company say, "There are just too many social media marketing businesses out there! It is impossible for us to be unique."

In some ways she is right. It is not easy to differentiate your business in a saturated market, but not impossible.

The challenge is not really coming from outside of your business, but inside. It is the mind-set, the culture, the unwillingness to move outside of comfort zones that is impacting the message of uniqueness.

So, while it may be true that there are a lot of social media marketing companies out there, the one thing that makes each of them unique is their story. None of them share the same story.

The story of your business – why it started, how it came about and what you have achieved - will always be a unique one.

In his book *The Storyteller's Secret: From TED Speakers to Business Legends, Why Some Ideas Catch On and Others Don't* [3], Carmine Gallo affirms that the ability to effectively tell your story is your ultimate competitive advantage and, by default, illustrates your uniqueness.

Gallo recommends a simple storytelling structure that can win over any audience. He explains how to craft a persuasive narrative and helps you develop your storytelling skills, enabling you to tell your unique story.

CHAPTER 6

THE PRINCIPLE OF FOCUS: MAPPING THE ROAD TO SUCCESS

> **"Always focus on the front windshield and not the rear-view mirror"**
> Colin Powell

Can you imagine what it would be like driving your car by looking in the rear-view mirror? That is definitely a disaster waiting to happen; yet this analogy is exactly the experience of many businesses.

Instead of concentrating on the vital few things that will enable the business to grow, leaders are constantly being distracted by decisions made in the past, the day-to-day problems, coming up with more and more ideas that are never brought to fruition, or concentrating on the wrong priorities and issues.

The result is that their focus and resources are diverted away from the road ahead; away from the activities that will lead to business growth.

In a small or medium-sized business, where resources are constrained, it is easier said than done to devote the time and attention required for strategy and execution. Yet, this is exactly why focus is imperative.

This chapter, therefore, centres on how to identify the few, vital issues and activities that will make the difference between growth and paralysis by analysis.

The Case for Relentless Focus

In his book *Think Big, Act Bigger*, Jeffrey Hayzlett [says], "what leaders struggle most to do is focus on what matters and ignore what doesn't matter".[4]

Hayzlett goes on to describe what he calls a dance between opportunity and distraction. This means identifying and applying strategies for maintaining focus on the things that will take the business from where it is now to where you want it to be.

Identify what matters

While the concept of relentless focus is readily understood and accepted, I have often found that the next challenge faced by leaders is to identify what, if given sufficient attention, will catapult business growth.

There are numerous tools that can help you to identify the most important things that you need to focus on to move your business forward. One well known and easy-to-use tool is the Balanced Business Scorecard[5].

Although originally invented by Kaplan and Norton in 1992 as a performance measurement tool, the Scorecard has been adapted for a variety of uses over the years. I have found that it adapts readily as a tool for identifying the areas that the business must focus on in order to achieve its growth targets.

Figure 7: The Balanced Business Scorecard

Customer	Financial
Human Resources	Internal Processes

VISION & MISSION

As illustrated above, the four areas of focus link directly to the vision and mission, against which the business can determine its success factors and develop key performance indicators for each area.

Selecting the Critical Few

Having identified the important things to focus on within the four areas described in the Balanced Business Scorecard, it is time to determine which of these to prioritise in order to maximise the potential for growth.

Everything cannot be priority. Prioritising is essential to focus your energy and attention on the things that really matter and to make the best use of your financial, human and operational resources.

You cannot put everything on hold in order to concentrate on business growth. Your existing customers still require and expect a high standard of service and your employees still need to be supported and developed.

Unless you can invest to bring about business growth, you must allocate resources to where they are most needed and most wisely targeted in order to free up the resources required.

For small to medium-sized businesses, it is best to concentrate efforts on a few, critical growth priorities. This allows you to carefully manage these priorities and to be agile enough to change tactics if the expected results are not being achieved within the timescale that you have determined.

At a simple level you can prioritise based on a variety of factors, including:

- Potential profitability
- Value to the customer
- Market penetration potential
- Speed to market
- Organisation capacity and capability

Prioritisation based on profitability is the most commonly used and rational basis for prioritisation and often provides the most easily measured results. Another option is to prioritise by involving colleagues and answering a few essential questions:

- What is one thing, or two or three things that, if we do them well, will definitively drive our business to achieve our growth targets?
- How will prioritising these one, two or three things guarantee that we achieve our goals?
- What behaviours do we need in the business to pursue these goals?
- How will we know when we are succeeding?
- Who will be responsible for each of these goals?
- When will we achieve these goals?

Concluding Thoughts

As a business leader, you probably have multiple priorities to juggle every day, but you cannot let that stop you from progressing and staying on track with your business vision.

There are many different strategies that you can put in play to help you stay focused and, therefore, allow you and others in the business to retain their focus. For example, you can:

1. Schedule it - intentionally set aside time to work *on*, rather than *in*, the business. One of my clients takes every Friday to just work on business growth. He works away from the office and his inbox and this allows him time to make sure he does not lose sight of the big picture.
2. Hire a coach or get a mentor – one of my clients actually has two coaches and several mentors that he schedules frequent check-ins with. Sometimes, to see and remain focused on what is important, you need to communicate with someone more experienced.
3. Learn from others – whatever challenges you are facing in growing your business, you can be sure that someone has trodden that road before you and has something to share about that experience. There are numerous books, articles, podcasts and videos that you can draw inspiration or get solutions from.
4. Hang out with the right people - surround yourself with people who believe in you and in what you are doing. Share your dreams and goals with others who you can trust to help you focus on the important, top line issue and keep you from wallowing in small, short-term details that you need to delegate to others on your team.

Business growth does not happen by accident. As a leader, you need to devote time, money and effort to achieving your goals. You cannot afford to be distracted, otherwise the goals that you have set will not be realised.

CHAPTER 7

THE PRINCIPLE OF TEAM: ACHIEVING MORE TOGETHER

> **"Interdependent people combine their own efforts with the efforts of others to achieve their greatest success"**
> STEPHEN COVEY

To grow a business requires teamwork at every level of the business.

Can you think of anything in life that you have achieved entirely on your own without any advice, guidance, help or support from anyone?

It is no different in business. Even if you are a sole trader, you need the help of others to successfully grow. This means having the right people, with the right skills, in the right place, at the right time. You need an actual (or a virtual) team with a range of skills, knowledge, experience and styles that complement your own.

This is not an easy feat.

This chapter focuses on:

- The role of the leader in the team;
- The team roles and styles that are necessary for every business and
- How to make sure that the team works

The Role of the leader

As the leader of the business you may want to, or even feel as if you have to, grow the business by yourself; but you cannot. You need a strong team, otherwise you will struggle and be crushed under the weight of growth.

Many leaders assume that they are best placed to spearhead the growth efforts of a company, but this is not always the case. We are all well aware of the need for the right type of leadership, depending on where the business is at in the Corporate Lifecycle as explored in Chapter 1.

One of the hardest things for a leader is to acknowledge that someone else might be better placed to lead the growth efforts. It takes courage to accept and let go of control, but remember that this is not the same as relinquishing your leadership role. You are maximising the potential for the company to achieve its growth objectives.

Having the confidence to let go and allow others to take the lead requires a level of trust and respect that cannot be obtained by accident. It must be nurtured over time and become part of the organisational culture. (See Chapter 8 – The Principle of Culture)

All leaders must be aware of their style and strengths, and surround themselves with people who can complement or compensate for their areas of weakness. Only by knowing what your leadership style and strengths are can you be confident in amassing a team of people with complementary styles and skills to your own.

The starting point is, therefore, to be clear about what you 'bring to the party'. If you don't already know your predominant style and skills, then you need to find out very quickly. There are numerous assessments and profiling tools that can help you identify your predominant style and strengths. The most well known of these include Myers Briggs Type Indicator (MBTI), DISC, Saville Wave and Margerison-McCann.

The Adizes Methodology, outlined in Chapter 2, identifies four main styles ad functions that are easily juxtaposed with most profiling tools. The four styles are summarised in this table:

Figure 8: Adizes Methodology Styles Summary

STYLES	STYLE AND ROLE
P Producer	Every company must produce results. This is the reason why they exist - to satisfy the needs of the customer. A Producer focuses on the necessary activities of producing the product or service being offered to the marketplace.
A Administrator	The Administering role focuses on how to do things. The Administrator focuses on the necessary activities of processing, organising and planning. This includes developing policies, procedures and systems.
E Entrepreneur	This is the role in the business that drives successful adaptation to change. The Entrepreneur focuses on the necessary activities of creating new opportunities or responding to threats. The Entrepreneur anticipates things that others cannot see, has vision and the willingness to undertake significant risks.
I Integrator	The Integrator role focuses on the development of a cohesive team that makes the organisation efficient in the long term. The Integrator focuses on the necessary activities of creating well-integrated organisations that have a culture of mutual trust and mutual respect.

No matter how skilled and experienced you are as a leader, it is impossible to be perfect in all four roles. You will naturally have a 'centre of gravity' or particular strength in one or two areas, very rarely in three, but never in all four.

Complementary and Diverse Teams

Every company needs a strong senior team to successfully grow the business. A strong team is both complementary and diverse. If the senior team has the same views, styles and experience, there will not be enough thoughtfulness on strategy and execution. On the other hand, dysfunctional teams can destroy businesses. The solution, therefore, is to create a diverse team with all four styles complementing each other.

Hiring people that are different from you as the founder or CEO can sometimes be difficult, but is very important. Once you've identified the right people with the range of different styles, skills and backgrounds, the challenge is to integrate these multiple differences because people with differing perspectives also have different approaches to things, and that can cause conflict.

The way to integrate these different styles, perspectives and approaches is to build mutual trust and respect within the team. However, this is easier said than done. Building mutual trust and respect takes time. In some instances it might require coaching, mentoring or facilitation to get everyone to a place where they can truly trust and respect their differences.

Entrepreneurial Behaviours

For a growing business, the Entrepreneur or 'E' role is vital, but must also be balanced with the P, A and I roles in the correct proportions.

The behaviours such as leading innovation, taking the initiative and being a risk taker are associated with the 'E' role and, when combined, become the greatest power for extraordinary business growth. Based on these entrepreneurial behaviours, growth-focused leaders inspire and energise their organisations to succeed.

How to make the team work

The way to make teams work – either the senior team or any other team in the business – is to create cohesion. Renowned author Patrick Lencioni[1] identifies 5 strategies for creating cohesive teams:

1. They trust one another
2. They engage in unfiltered conflict around ideas
3. They commit to decisions and plans of action
4. They hold one another accountable for delivering against those plans
5. They focus on achieving collective results

The five strategies above require a constructive and disciplined process for solving problems and decision-making, both of which will be addressed later in this book.

Concluding Thoughts

In business, there is a significant difference between the performance of a group of people working together and the achievements of a fully synchronised team. When a team is synchronised they share a common purpose. They share a level of trust, respect and accountability that enables them as a tight-knit group of people to passionately work towards and achieve something exceptional.

It is not easy to attain and sustain perfect synchronisation, but when you have a group of talented, committed people you can achieve far more than you imagined. A synchronised team is not just talented, smart, motivated people achieving their numbers and meeting deadlines. It is a team creating something that is greater than any one or two of them could ever do alone. Growth-focused businesses understand this and they must create teams of distinction to leverage the power of collaboration to achieve their individual and collective best.

CHAPTER 8

THE PRINCIPLE OF CULTURE: SHAPING ATTITUDES, BELIEFS AND BEHAVIOURS

> **"Corporate culture is the only sustainable competitive advantage that is completely within the control of the entrepreneur"**
> DAVID CUMMINS, CO-FOUNDER, PARDOT

If you think that organisational culture is an intangible, soft concept that has no bearing on business growth and success, think again. Many of the problems experienced by businesses have to do with organisational culture.

According to a Human Capital Trends Survey of more than 3, 300 business leaders by Deloitte in 2015,[1] organisational culture is the most important issue that companies around the world face because it has a direct effect on performance, profit and loss, balance sheet and other financial indicators. The survey found that 87% of organisations cite culture as one of their top challenges with more than half of the business leaders rating this issue as "urgent".

Defining organisational culture

If you distil the numerous definitions, essentially organisational culture is the personality or soul of the company, comprising:

- The organisation's values
- The behaviours and standard of conduct (the way everyone acts, thinks and speaks) associated with these values
- The expression of the values and behaviours in customer interactions, the business brand, and written and oral communications

In essence, culture is the mental make-up of the business and is considered to be the decisive factor in obtaining success.

How organisational cultures develop

To understand the culture of an organisation and its development, it is important to analyse its history, its contexts, its traumas and how these influence the way that it deals with external influences or change. Even though the historical context of the company's 'birth' may have been useful in the beginning, it can become a hindrance if the organisation sticks to it in spite of the changing environment.

How organisational culture is sustained

Eventually organisational culture becomes self-sustaining through socialisation. In other words, 'this is the way we do things around here'. Whether good or bad, socialisation of culture is often reflected in repetitive phrases and sayings such as:

> 'We tried that before and it doesn't work'
> 'Here, we dress casually'
> 'Just follow the rules, no matter what, otherwise life isn't worth living'
> 'We each take ownership for solving customer problems'
> 'We always work together to solve problems'

Identifying organisational culture problems

Organisational culture becomes a problem when the way in which the organisation usually operates puts obstacles in the way of achieving its goals and targets, including growth.

Examples of organisational culture problems include:

- An internal orientation and wasted energy on politics, conflict and performance issues rather than the external orientation required for business growth
- A lack of transparency and accountability coupled with a perception of favouritism amongst certain groups or individuals
- Lack of mutual trust and respect characterised by a tendency to avoid teamwork, not speaking up and following rules to the letter

Changing organisational culture

Changing the personality of an organisation is very difficult.

Despite this understanding of culture and the many studies and books written over decades to demonstrate the link between culture, performance and success, the fact remains that many culture-change efforts fail or fall short of their potential.

But the good news is that successful culture transformation is possible if there is an integrated approach that addresses four key principles:

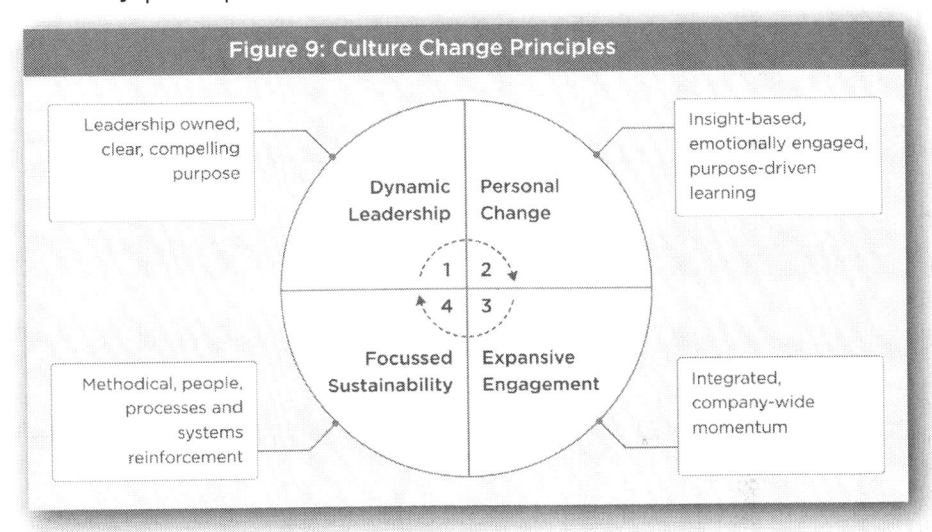

Figure 9: Culture Change Principles

- Leadership owned, clear, compelling purpose — **Dynamic Leadership (1)**
- Insight-based, emotionally engaged, purpose-driven learning — **Personal Change (2)**
- Integrated, company-wide momentum — **Expansive Engagement (3)**
- Methodical, people, processes and systems reinforcement — **Focussed Sustainability (4)**

This disciplined approach will result in a strong culture where everyone in the business understands what it means and is inspired to do what it takes to be more innovative, joined-up, deliver outstanding services, embrace opportunities and ultimately grow the business.

The holistic approach must be sequenced in a manner that your business will gain the most from. However, change programmes cannot be delivered in a linear fashion. There will inevitably be overlap between the phases. There will also need to be flexibility to re-sequence or adjust the approach, depending on organisational requirements, resources and the progress of the implementation.

Organisational culture is the outcome of a lasting process in which the attitude, beliefs and behaviour of people are gradually shaped and is always a logical adaptation to a changed environment. If the organisational culture is blocking success, then a change of culture has to be considered. To be successful, therefore, leaders must be aware of their own readiness for change, set and exemplify the organisational values, and align reward systems to the desired culture.

Concluding Thoughts

Organisational culture impacts every aspect of a business from the way people think, feel and act to the customer experience, productivity levels and bottom-line profitability.

If culture is neglected, the impact on both tangible and intangible factors produces a high failure rate for change, growth or improvement activities.

It is, therefore, one of leaders' prime tasks to define, exemplify and inculcate the organisational culture that will bring about growth-producing change.

When you grasp the power of the cultural dynamics of business you quickly realise that the amount of energy and attention you give to organisational culture have more far-reaching and long-lasting benefits than almost any other leadership activity.

CHAPTER 9

The Principle of Problem-Solving: Moving Forward Unfettered

> **"We cannot solve our problems with the same level of thinking that created them"**
> Albert Einstein

In addition to dealing with change, one of the major challenges that growth-focused businesses face is resolving the entrenched, thorny problems that are preventing them from moving forward.

Many people see the leader as the 'problem-solver' and expect him or her to have the answers to whatever the issue may be. Of course, this is not feasible or desirable for any progressive business. Everyone, at every level of the company, should be confident to take responsibility for solving problems. This is the only way to ensure that the business is agile, encourages accountability and creates a culture of innovation.

Any problem, whether it is financial, operational or human resource related, requires, at minimum, five important steps:

Figure 10: Problem Solving Process

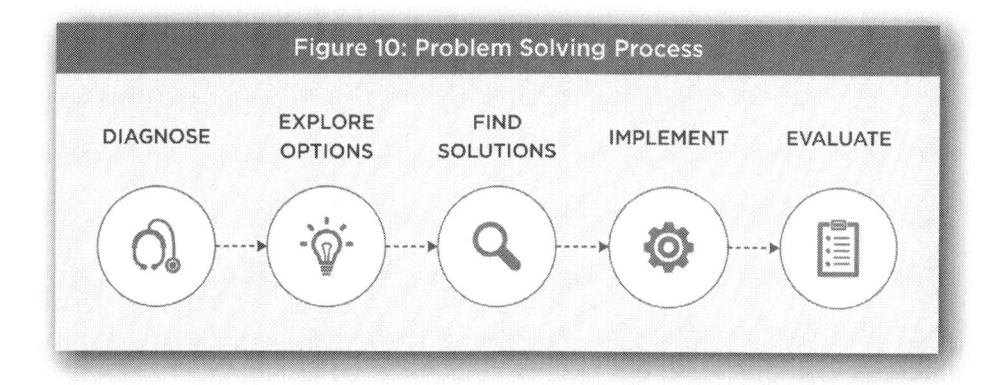

DIAGNOSE → EXPLORE OPTIONS → FIND SOLUTIONS → IMPLEMENT → EVALUATE

Jumping directly to solutions without defining the problem and exploring a range of options for addressing it is counter-productive. Conversely, diagnosing a problem and then implementing solutions before exploring a full range of options will not result in the right answer either.

We already know from Chapter 2 that even when you have found solutions to problems the result is more problems. This is a dynamic of change and it is ceaseless, so problem-solving must also be a dynamic process.

The fact that hundreds of tools and processes have been invented to tackle problem-solving in business attests to the fact that this is an important skill and one that is imperative for business growth.

As with any of the tools that I refer to in this book, most cannot be followed in a mechanistic, linear fashion. There will be overlap and some activities will demand more resources than others.

The important thing to understand is that it is virtually impossible to grow a business that is bogged down with unresolved problems. Every business that has growth ambitions must be as adept at solving problems as it is at managing change, innovating, delivering customer service excellence or any of the other fundamental factors addressed in this book.

This chapter, therefore, focuses on tackling each of the problem-solving steps illustrated in Figure 10 above.

Finding the Cause of the Problem

Your approach to diagnosing the problem will be determined by a number of factors including its complexity, the age of the problem, the resources at your disposal and the timescale that you are working with.

The aim of this first stage is to identify the root cause of a problem. The process must drive you to find what the actual problem is, rather than just its symptoms.

The diagnostic phase is just the same as a visit to the doctor – you have some symptoms but the doctor's role is to determine what is causing the symptom in order to find the right solution. A headache can be caused by anything from tiredness to a brain tumour. A prescription for a painkiller is not going to be of any use if the cause of the headache is an abnormal growth on the brain!

In business, you run the risk of wasting time and money solving the symptoms and not the cause of the problem. While this is happening, a gulf is being created between you and your competitors as they correctly diagnose and address the problems, enabling them to introduce new products or services into the marketplace and to grow rapidly.

By seeking to solve the underlying cause, you are aiming to ensure that the problem does not reoccur, and if it does, that it is dealt with quickly. This will ultimately save you time, money and effort.

There are numerous problem-diagnosis tools that are readily available for your use. One of the most well-known, easy-to-use and methodical of these is the "5 Whys" which was developed by Sakichi Toyoda in 1930[1] and became so popular that it is still being used to solve problems today.

Generating and Exploring Options

Just as the challenge is to identify the underlying cause of the problem, the temptation to move into solution mode without generating and exploring a variety of options can also lead to the wrong solution.

One guaranteed way to generate diverse, good quality options is based on the work of Dr Ichak Adizes.

The Adizes Methodology has proved, for more than 40 years, that bringing together a diverse group of people, each with a distinctive view of the problem, will produce much better options that are usually easier to implement because the people affected by the decisions were involved in creating the solutions.

The need to involve people with a varied view of the problem was addressed in Chapter 7 where we identified the four P, A, E, I styles and functions required in any successful business.

These are just as relevant for decision-making, which we will look at in the next chapter.

Finding Solutions

It is accepted wisdom that solution finding generally employs a brainstorming approach involving a variety of people who will look at the issue from multiple perspectives. The aim is to generate as any solutions as possible, particularly novel, new or unconventional approaches. Be open-minded and prepared to consider solutions that may initially seem infeasible.

This is an opportunity to be creative and not to become bogged down at this early stage of the process with whether or not the solutions are feasible. The solution finding process can be enjoyable and include the added benefit of creating cohesion amongst team members. It is also worth keeping in mind that it may not be possible to find solutions for every aspect of the issue. When this is the case, break the issue down and try to generate solutions for all of the different issues.

Implementing Solutions

This step is simple - choose a solution or solutions from the previous step and take action. To choose a solution, you need to weigh the pros and cons of each potential solution. Many businesses will pursue solutions that are associated with low risk and that are compatible with priorities and future goals.

Evaluating Outcomes

Having implemented a solution, the final stage is to evaluate how successful it was and also what was not successful. If the solution did not completely address the issue, you can then review some of the different solutions presented in the earlier stages of the process.

Concluding Thoughts

The well-being of a business depends on the work being effectively performed and, in order to do this, we must successfully address the day-to-day and the strategic problems that inevitably arise in every company.

The work of leaders is largely to make decisions. Decision-making is only effective when you know which issue requires attention and being open to step outside of your comfort zone to find the best solutions.

The abilities and skills that determine the quality of our decisions and solutions are stored not only in the brain of leaders, but also in the brains of customers, staff and even competitors.

One of the most effective solution finding approaches I came across was in a not-for-profit business that was looking for answers outside of their sector and industry. Not only did this raise the level of their strategic thinking, it also produced some innovative partnerships that attracted resources they would never have dreamt of.

While I am a staunch advocate for involving people at all levels of the business in problem-solving, there is also much to be said for seeking external solutions in business sectors that are very different from your own.

CHAPTER 10

THE PRINCIPLE OF DECISION-MAKING: THE POWER OF CHOOSING

> **"Whenever you see a successful business, someone once made a courageous decision."**
> PETER F. DRUCKER

Whenever we reach a crossroads and are faced with the choice of whether to turn left, right, go straight ahead or turn around, making good choices determines how successful we will be.

Growing businesses are faced with numerous choices arising from either problems or opportunities on a daily basis and the secret to their success is synonymous with the effectiveness of their decision-making. Decision-making can be very hard because it requires selecting a solution where the positives outweigh the potential negatives and this often results in some level of conflict or dissatisfaction, regardless of what decision is made.

Making decisions in an ever-changing, ambiguous context may tempt you into avoiding decisions. But the reality is that the only way to stay in control of your success is to make the best possible decisions that you can.

It is much easier, and more likely to be effective, if you have a transparent and proven decision-making process that encourages collaborative solution finding concurrent with clarity of vision, mission and focus.

Decision-making Models

The myriad of decision-making tools that have been developed over many decades attests to the fact that decision-making is not an easy thing for businesses to do. While there can be no guarantee that these tools will lead to the right decision, they do assist individuals, teams and the businesses as a whole to make the best possible decisions.

It is important, therefore, that you find a decision-making process that aligns with your business culture, context and approach. This means taking the time to research, understand and identify the different models and approaches that are available.

This is made easier by the fact that decision-making is categorised into one of three models:

1. The Rational (Classical) Model
2. The Administrative (Bounded Rationality) Model
3. The Retrospective Decision-Making Model.

- The Rational (Classical) Model relies on structured, methodical thinking that makes use of quantitative

data such as financial performance reports, and the application of logic to assess business choices in order make decisions.
- The Administrative (Bounded Rationality) Model is based on the rational model, but also recognises the human constraints and limitations of time, cognitive abilities, clarity and availability of information in order to make effective decisions.
- The Retrospective Model is quite simply justifying an intuitive decision after it has already been made.

Debate continues to rage as to which of these models is most effective and there are pros and cons for each. The important lesson for any small or medium-sized enterprise that is seeking to grow is that decision-making is a vital principle of business growth.

Decision-making Processes

A common feature of all three models is that they follow the same core stages. They also mirror the steps in problem-solving because problem-solving and decision-making go hand in hand.

Depending on the decision-making model selected, you will find that some have either expanded or contracted these steps. However, there is consistency and similarity in approach, with these 6 stages at the core of most of them:

Figure 11: Six Step Decision Making Model

STAGE 1	Describe the specific decision to be taken
STAGE 2	Collate all relevant information relating to the decision to be taken
STAGE 3	Bring together a decision making team to explore options
STAGE 4	Explore a range of options and make the decision
STAGE 5	Assign responsibilities and implement the decision
STAGE 6	Review impact and outcomes

The Decision-Making Team

The simple rule of thumb for good decision-making is to identify who will be impacted by a decision downstream and involve them in the decision-making process upstream.

Giving everyone in the business the opportunity to genuinely participate in a decision-making process not only helps to create a better decision through their unique insights, but also makes it easier to implement the decision itself because they feel a greater sense of ownership and less resistance to change.

While it is neither time– nor cost-effective to involve everyone in the decision-making process, it is important to make every effort to include those who will be impacted by the decision.

Keep in mind that growing the business is the most important element of your decision-making process. Therefore, gather your team together to make decisions that will help you achieve those objectives. Even better, motivate your team to come up with solutions that will improve those objectives.

They say that two heads are better than one, so imagine what a whole lot of brains can do!

Concluding Thoughts

There are three common habits that I have noticed in relation to decision-making.

The first is that business leaders often rely on intuition, gut feeling or precedence to make even the most vital strategic decisions. Whilst this can sometimes produce a positive outcome, more often than not, if the proper time, attention and systematic approach had been devoted to making decisions, there would be less time and money wasted trying to undo the effects of poorly-made decisions.

The second habit is not making decisions in a timely manner. I advocate the application of the Eisenhower Principle[1] which stipulates that there are only two types of decisions- the urgent and the important. You will be aware that this principle is usually applied to time management, but I believe it works just as well for decision-making.

When making decisions, leaders must be savvy about the difference between the decisions that need to be made immediately and those that need to be pondered over a period of time.

The third decision-making habit of leaders is to be involved in all decision-making. Not only does this stymie the growth and progression of others in the business, but also it usually dampens their commitment and allows them to abdicate responsibility for any decisions made.

I pointed out to one of the leaders that I worked with that not only was he deciding whether or not to pursue a multi-million dollar deal, he was also involved in decisions about what colour the toilet paper should be. How can the business grow effectively with this type of decision-making approach?

CHAPTER 11

THE PRINCIPLE OF INNOVATION: DRIVING BUSINESS GROWTH

> "When you think there is nothing left to improve on, your business dies, for there is no shortage of innovators"
>
> BANGAMBIKI HABYARIMANA

One of my first clients was a company that developed software management solutions for engineering firms in the oil and gas sector. They were doing phenomenally well and grew exponentially, having secured some very large clients that are amongst the world's elite in the industry.

With major contracts from such prestigious companies, they could be forgiven for assuming that the growth experienced by the company would continue. They were so successful that one of their competitors, a much larger, international company, instigated talks to buy them. For the owners, this was beyond their wildest dreams and would see their planned exit strategy come to fruition in a matter of a few years and allow them to amass unprecedented personal wealth.

However, on the brink of completing the deal, the largest of their customers decided to dramatically reduce the contracted services that they had with my client, leaving only two small ones in place. The attractiveness and security of these large customers was one of the main reasons why the purchase of my client's company had been contemplated in the first instance.

With this change of context, the takeover deal was soon withdrawn, leaving my client in serious trouble with no apparent solution to their financial problems. Despite this major blow which left them without a buyer and without their major customer, this small company understood the principle of innovation and business growth (which is how they started in the first place). Rather than withdraw, licking their wounds, they began to innovate again. Innovation was not a magic bullet for them. It took time, a great deal of effort and personal investment in the company to recover from these unexpected blows. Today, they are even more successful than ever before. They have expanded into new sectors and are operating an international company in Europe, Asia and Australia with further opportunities emerging in the Middle East.

Essentially, innovation is about change, as we explored in Chapter 2 of this book. Innovation is the ability to adapt, to change, to anticipate changing customer needs or desires and bring timely, effective solutions to address those needs or desires.

The Innovation Myth

The capability to innovate and to bring innovation successfully to market is a crucial determinant of business success, whatever the size of the company.

There is growing awareness among small and medium-sized enterprises that innovation isn't an optional extra; it is unquestionably one of the main drivers of business vitality, growth and competitiveness.

As well as being a critical factor in meeting the challenge of operating in globalised markets, innovation moved to centre-stage in economic policymaking in countries that realise that there is a desperate need for a logical, co-ordinated approach to encouraging and supporting businesses to become more innovative. Yet, despite these realisations, innovation is still considered by many to be the preserve of large, technology-focused companies based on the misguided belief that innovation is purely a "blue ocean" activity.

Nothing could be further from the truth. There is a continuum of innovation as depicted below:

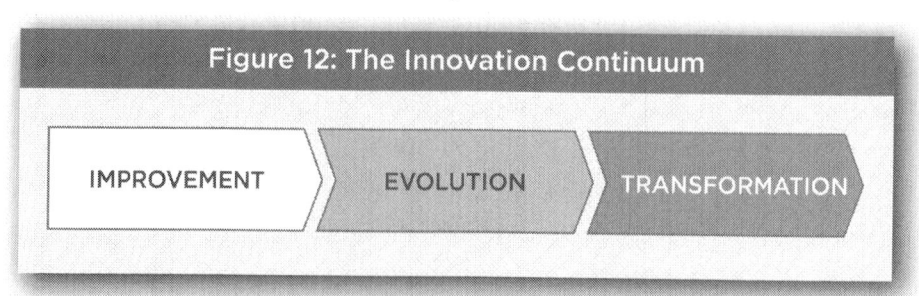

Figure 12: The Innovation Continuum

IMPROVEMENT → EVOLUTION → TRANSFORMATION

At one end the continuum is small, incremental innovations. This usually means taking an existing process, product or service and tweaking it to make it a little better. An example of an incremental innovation might be to reduce the response time for following up customer complaints.

Improvement is about low-risk innovation that requires little or no upfront investment, but will provide a good return.

At the other end of the continuum is transformation, which is about radical, all-encompassing change. This usually means creating a new product or service, or bringing something new into a sparsely occupied marketplace where there is little or no competition – a "blue ocean".

Transformational innovation usually requires upfront investment in development, testing and marketing of the product or service to determine its potential success. This is high-risk innovation and carries no guarantee of success.

In the middle is evolutionary innovation. This focuses again on an existing product or service, but rather than small, incremental improvements, there is development or progression to the next iteration. This could be adding a feature such as an HD camera to a smart phone or offering 100% money-back guarantee of satisfaction.

While this is a lower-risk approach to innovation as the product or service is already known and succeeding in the marketplace, some level of investment is still required and again there is no guarantee of success.

The two ends of the innovation continuum are very different in nature and it is important to understand the unique properties of each in order to determine where it is most advantageous for you to devote resources.

Mission-Driven Innovation

Wherever you choose to focus your innovation efforts, there is one question that must underpin your decision: Is this new way of doing things going to substantially assist your ability to deliver on your mission?

While it is true that innovation, whether incremental or transformational, is changing the status quo, the soul of your company – the mission - must not change.

Many companies make the mistake of using the term "diversification" to completely and radically shift from one activity to another. This is not innovation and can lead to spectacular failure.

It makes little sense for a shoe manufacturer to diversify into making scuba diving gear! Although there will inevitably be individuals who love both shoes and scuba diving, I am not convinced that these are two activities that one should choose to do at the same time.

Such a departure from the business mission, quite rightly, calls into question the reason for its existence. If you are a shoe manufacturer that is into scuba diving, I would suggest that the solution is to create another business with a clear mission, vision and value proposition.

You may have some overlap in core services such as financial or human resource management, but trying to amalgamate two very different business missions rarely succeeds.

Innovation Culture

While having a mission-driven innovation is important, of equal importance is the need for businesses in all sectors and of all sizes to create an environment in which everyone in the business can and is encouraged to contribute to innovation.

Building a culture that supports innovation can help your business stay relevant, meet challenges and stay competitive. Innovation is not just about new ideas, but also about new ways of applying ideas and it is usually the people who are closest to the customer and product or service that have the best ideas.

As a business leader, you can encourage innovation by asking staff how they would improve the way they do their job, using business strategies that welcome innovation, reviewing current processes and arranging regular training and networking opportunities for all staff.

You can resource innovation by giving your staff the space, time and money to focus on being creative.

An innovation culture is one that embraces change, encourages creativity, values teamwork, is willing to take risks and avoids blame when ideas don't work.

Concluding Thoughts

Far from being the domain of a few select companies, innovation can and does take place in a variety of organisations, regardless of size, sector or type of business.

Many small and medium-sized enterprises will shy away from using the word "innovation" because they do not believe that it applies to them. This is because they define innovation as invention, creating something brand new that has never been seen before.

Whenever I work with companies that are stuck because they cannot envisage themselves as being innovative, we simply agree to substitute the word innovation for one that they are more comfortable with. Some have chosen to use the word "creativity", whilst others prefer to call it "problem-solving".

Whatever the word selected, the important thing is that everyone in the business understands the importance of coming up with new ideas for improving what is being done or meeting a customer need that is not being satisfied.

Call it what you like, but every small and medium-sized enterprise that is seeking to grow must also be innovating.

CHAPTER 12

THE PRINCIPLE OF RISK MANAGEMENT: TAKING THE LEAP

>"**The only safe thing is to take a chance**"
>
>ELAINE MAY

A few years ago I attended a retreat to enjoy some space and time to focus on and make some decisions about the future direction of my life and my business.

One of the activities was to climb a rope ladder to a small platform, grasp a zip wire and jump off the platform. It was a 300-foot drop and I am scared of heights!

You can imagine that I was not too keen on the idea, but I managed to convince myself to go for it. To my absolute shock and amazement it was not only the thought of standing on a platform 300 feet off the ground that intimidated me, but also the thought of climbing up the rope ladder caused a tremendous fear to build up inside me!

This experience taught me three very salutary lessons about business growth that I have since applied to my own business and also used to help many of the business leaders that I work with. I will share them with you in this chapter.

Lesson 1: You Have to Climb

One of the main reasons why small and medium-sized enterprises fail to grow is the reluctance of the leaders to take a chance to even begin the journey towards growth. There is such a fear of making mistakes or failing that some leaders will never make the step towards growth.

Unless you take the first steps to where you want to be, you will forever be looking at the horizon to what could have been and wondering what you could have achieved if only you had started the climb.

Just as I had to climb the rope ladder to get to the platform where the zip line was located, so it is for small and medium-sized enterprises. The platform that you need to get to is high off the ground and the only way to get there is to make the climb. The climb in this analogy, therefore, represents the journey which every small and medium-sized enterprise must take in order to get to a position where it is ready to pursue growth.

The journey itself is the understanding and application of the principles set out in this book which are the most important areas to address when preparing for growth.

Lesson 2: Take the Leap

Once I conquered my fears and began to climb that rope ladder, I was still afraid because I was getting higher and higher and the rope ladder was swaying all over the place so I didn't feel secure.

But I did it and there I was looking at the ground below, which was where I so desperately wanted to be. The problem was that I couldn't go back down the ladder as people were coming up behind me and having put all of that effort into the climb, it seemed ridiculous to try to go back the way I came anyway.

Just as in life and business, once you know, you have to do something with that knowledge. You cannot return to a place of ignorance or oblivion. You're here now so there's nothing left to do but jump.

Now that you know what you need to do to prepare your small or medium-sized enterprise for growth, the only thing left to do is jump.

Although taking the journey cannot guarantee you success, your chances of achieving your goals are increased a hundredfold because you made the climb. Even after you've climbed the ladder, growth is still a leap of faith.

The platform can also be a frightening place to be, especially if you're looking back at what it took to get there. But remember that there is a zip wire and you have a harness – just make sure that both are in good working order. In other words, make sure that you have a good strategy for mitigation and management of the risks associated with growth and you can jump with a high degree of confidence that not only will you survive, but you will thrive and maybe even enjoy the leap.

Lesson 3: You are Not Alone
The road towards business growth is a well-travelled one and the many thousands of leaders that have taken this journey before have left some very clear signposts so that you do not fall into the same potholes that they did.

When I was making the climb and as I prepared to take the leap from the platform, I was being encouraged, cajoled and cheered on by my team that was managing the activity and also my fellow participants on the retreat.

I realised that, despite my fears, I was not making this journey alone. I had other people around me who were interested in my success and so do you. There are business coaches, business support organisations, fellow entrepreneurs, investors and even family and friends who will lend their support and are committed to helping your business succeed.

Managing Risk
In the face of this tumultuous business landscape, the instinct might be to wait, to hold steady to see if the storm will

subside. But almost nine years on from the global financial crisis, the business landscape still has not returned to what it was and nor is it likely to. The uncertainty we see today may well be the new normal. Therefore, the ability to make strategic decisions in volatile, ambiguous conditions has become a business imperative. Doing so swiftly and having the ability to influence and, as far as possible, control risk in this environment will be the defining factors for business growth.

Small to medium-sized businesses are exposed to internal and external risks all the time, but sound risk management can reduce the chance of a particular event taking place and, if it does take place, sound risk management can also reduce its impact.

Risk is defined as the probability of an event and its consequences. Risk management is the practice of using processes, methods and tools for managing these risks. Risk management focuses on identifying what could go wrong, evaluating which risks should be dealt with and implementing strategies to deal with them. Businesses that identify risks will be better prepared for dealing with them.

Caisse's Risk Model[1] depicted below provides a succinct and comprehensive description of the three categories to identify the risk factors associated with business growth:

Figure 13: The Caisse's Risk Model

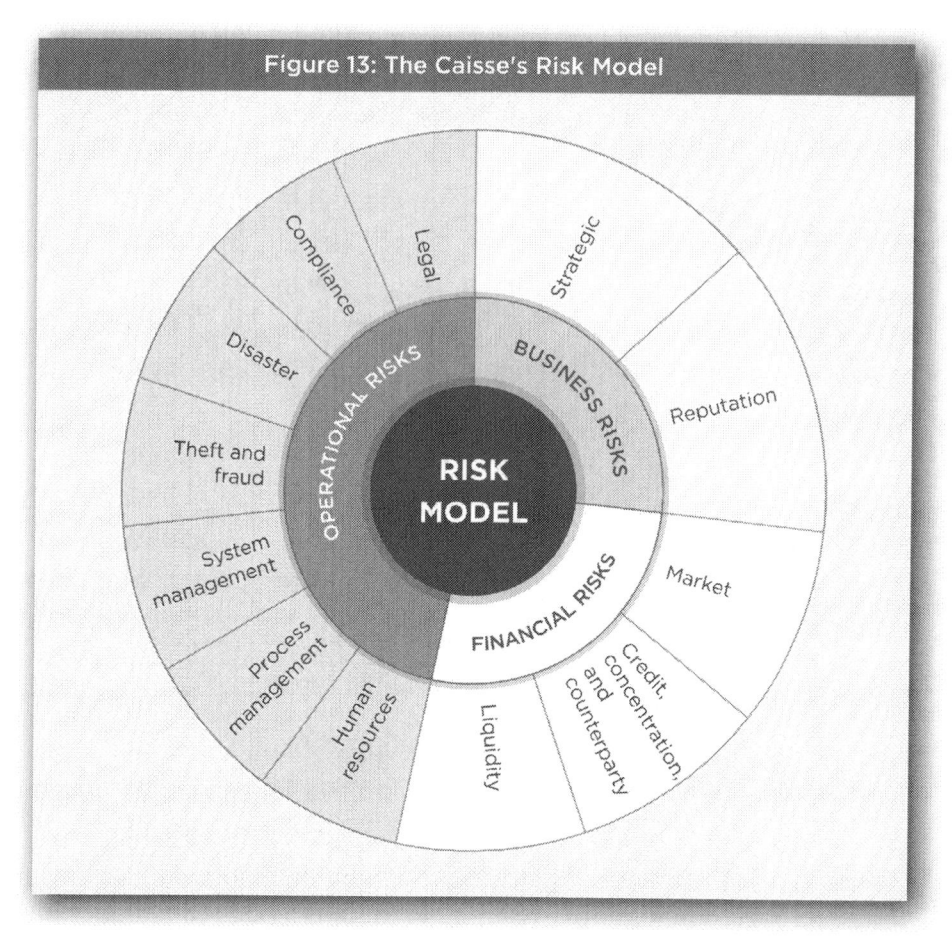

Operational Risks: Compliance, Legal, Disaster, Theft and fraud, System management, Process management, Human resources

Business Risks: Strategic, Reputation

Financial Risks: Market, Credit concentration and counterparty, Liquidity

While it may not be feasible for a small business to address all of these risks, when preparing your business for growth, carrying out risk analysis in the following areas of the company is a minimum:

- Accounting and financial management policies and practices
- Sales and marketing
- Business continuity
- Supply chain

- Human resources
- Internal controls covering policies and procedures
- Insurances
- The regulatory environment that your business operates in

Once you have done this, develop a risk mitigation plan and programme to effectively manage these risks, reduce the possibility of failure and increase your business' chances of success.

Business growth comes at a price, and understanding the associated risks and rewards of growth is essential for small and medium-sized enterprises.

Concluding Thoughts

Small and medium-sized enterprise business leaders are generally positive about their prospects for growth and have realistic expectations about the level of growth they can achieve. Their desire for growth is not simply a means to improve the bottom-line, with many business leaders believing that a larger business is better able to deal with market volatility, change and crisis.

Over the years I have also found that some businesses are willing to take significant risks in order to grow, even though they know that it challenges their survival. Another common experience is that leaders view impediments to growth as lying outside their organisations with risks such as weak demand and low availability of skilled employees being the major concerns.

Whatever your growth ambitions, as a leader, it is vital to focus on both the internal and external constraints that produce undesirable consequences for achieving growth.

Ensure that your risk identification and mitigation plans are well thought out and realistic. It is good to be ambitious, but not at any cost.

WHAT NEXT? - OVER TO YOU

"Things may come to those who wait, but only the things left by those who hustle."
ABRAHAM LINCOLN

This book has introduced and discussed a range of important principles that small and medium-sized enterprises need to acquire in order to successfully prepare and position themselves for growth.

After an initial period of doubt and apprehension, most business leaders find that, if properly applied, these principles help them to avoid costly errors and make the transition from small or medium to large much more efficient and effective. The risk of failure is reduced and there is a great deal of scope for learning from other similar businesses.

Many businesses embark on a journey of growth without any preparation. Unfortunately, most fail, but they don't have to. Help is at hand.

If you would like help to implement these principles, we offer a variety of educational, consultancy, leadership and coaching programmes tailored to your specific needs.

We would also like to give anyone who has purchased this book the opportunity to receive a free business growth assessment – visit www.getfitforgrowth.com to find out how fit your business is for growth.

The 12 growth principles are based on experience and practice, not mere theory. Application of these principles will yield a return on investment in the form of enhanced profits and achievement of your growth plans.

I hope you will use this book to guide your journey to growth. The principles can be revisited for each stage of your growth journey or simply transferred and applied to your own mounting experience in the years to come.

Planning and managing change is and will remain crucial to business growth, but this must start with leadership. The way that you lead the business will enhance or hinder preparations for growth. Try to stand back and examine your leadership approach.

This book has been written to help raise your awareness as a business leader or owner, so remember that you are the fulcrum around which the growth of the business will pivot.

We are also here to help if you need any hands-on support to implement these principles.

Good luck!

About the Author

Barbara E. Armstrong

As a business consultant, executive coach, and speaker, Barbara Armstrong specializes in developing successful leaders and accomplishing transformational change for businesses. Having created programs over the years for a range of businesses of every size, both national and international, Barbara has a reputation for knowing how to move successful businesses forward, promoting cohesion and synergy between business goals and values.

Barbara is an Adizes Methodology™ certified consultant with a postgraduate diploma in management studies and a professional certification in management. Barbara also has several coaching qualifications and many other business certifications and honours to her name.

She is the founder and leader of her own business with offices in the UK and Barbados, and she hopes to expand to the United States in the coming years. She is married and has five children and four grandchildren.

NOTES

Preface

1. Marshall Goldsmith and Mark Reiter, *What Got You Here Won't Get You There: How Successful People Become Even More Successful.* (New York: Hachette Books, 2007).

Introduction

2. Marshall Goldsmith and Mark Reiter, *What Got You Here Won't Get You There: How Successful People Become Even More Successful.* (New York: Hachette Books, 2007).

3. View the following websites to learn more about Dr. Adizes and his work: http://www.ichakadizes.com, http://www.adizes.com.

Chapter 1

1. "Field of Dreams", directed by: Phil Aden Robinson (1989; California: Universal Pictures).

Chapter 2

1. Henry Ford's quote: http://www.goodreads.com/quotes/904186-if-you-always-do-what-you-ve-always-done-you-ll-always

2. Dr Ichak Adizes, Managing Corporate Lifecycles, (California: Adizes Institute Publishing, 2004).

Chapter 3

1. Ajaero Tony Martin, "How to Learn From Your Mistakes in Business", http://www.mytopbusinessideas.com/learning-from-your-mistakes/

2. James Altucher, *The Choose Yourself Guide to Wealth*, (CreateSpace Independent Publishing Platform: 2015), p. 45.

3. Dr. Asmus Komm et al, "Return on Leadership – Competencies that Generate Growth," Egon Zehnder International and McKinsey & Company, (2011). Accessed June 25, 2016. http://www.egonzehnder.com/files/return_on_leadership.pdf

Chapter 4

4. Lewis Carroll, "Alice's Adventures in Wonderland & Through the Looking-Glass" https://www.goodreads.com/quotes/

5. Simon Sinek, *Start With The Why*, (New York: The Penguin Group, 2009).

6. Darrell K. Rigby, "Management Tools 2015: An Executive's Guide", (Boston: Bain & Company, Inc, 2015). http://www.bain.com/Images/BAIN_GUIDE_Management_Tools_2015_executives_guide.pdf

7. John Kotter, "When CEOs Talk Strategy, 70% of the Company Doesn't Get It." Forbes. Last Modified: July 9, 2013. http://www.forbes.com/sites/johnkotter/2013/07/09/heres-why-ceo-strategies-fall-on-deaf-ears/#7b82d1421ea7

Chapter 5

1. "What is An USP Unique Selling Proposition and Why Do I Want or Need One". Coaching by Subject Experts. http://www.coachingbysubjectexperts.com/what-is-an-usp/

2. Jill Konarth, "Value Proposition Examples – Words that Get Meetings". http://www.jillkonrath.com/sales-blog/bid/140981/Value-Proposition-Examples-Words-That-Get-Meetings

3. Carmine Gallo, *The Storyteller's Secret: From TED Speakers to Business Legends, Why Some Ideas Catch On and Others Don't* (New York: St. Martin's Press, 2016).

Chapter 6

4. Jeffrey Hayzlett, *Think Big, Act Bigger: The Rewards of Being Relentless* (California: Entrepreneurship Press, 2015).

5. Visit the official website of the Balance Scorecard Institute to learn more about the Balance Business Scorecard: http://balancedscorecard.org/Resources/About-the-Balanced-Scorecard

Chapter 7

1. Patrick Lencioni, *The Five Dysfunctions of a Team: A Leadership Fable* (California: Josse-Bass, 2002).

Chapter 8

1. "Global Human Capital Trends 2015," (Deloitte University Press, 2015). http://www2.deloitte.com/content/dam/Deloitte/at/Documents/human-capital/hc-trends-2015.pdf.

Chapter 9

1. Visit the following website to learn more about Toyoda's "5 Whys" concept: https://www.mindtools.com/pages/article/newTMC_5W.htm

Chapter 10

1. Visit the following website to learn more about the Eisenhower Principle: concept: https://www.mindtools.com/pages/article/newHTE_91.htm

Chapter 12

1. Visit the following website to learn more about The Caisse Risk Model: http://cdpq.com/en/investments/risk-management

Made in the USA
Charleston, SC
12 November 2016